READING
CHANGED MY LIFE!

THREE
TRUE
STORIES

Beth Johnson

 THE TOWNSEND LIBRARY

Reading Changed My Life!
Three True Stories

TP THE TOWNSEND LIBRARY

For more titles in the Townsend Library,
visit our website: **www.townsendpress.com**

Photography:
Maria Cárdenas by Paul Kowal
Daisy Russell by Beth Johnson
Julia Burney by Mark Hertzberg

Townsend Press, Inc.
1038 Industrial Drive
West Berlin, New Jersey 08091

ISBN 1-59194-012-5

Library of Congress Control Number:
2003102664

Contents

Introduction

The three women whose stories appear in this book have never met. They live in three different states: Florida, Missouri, and Wisconsin. They have made their livings in different ways: one as a farm laborer, one as a factory worker, and one as a police officer. They come from three different racial groups: Hispanic, white, and African-American.

But for all their differences, Maria Cárdenas, Daisy Russell, and Julia Burney share a very important characteristic. Each knows how painful it is to be a non-reader in today's world. Two of them know that pain from personal experience; the third knows it from observing the pain of those around her.

These three women share other qualities as well. For one thing, each of them has lived with violence, abuse, and poverty. The bad things that have happened to them are sometimes difficult to read about. In spite of the pain they have suffered, they have each, in their different ways, said, "This stops with me." They have refused to do to others what was once done to them. They have taken hard, courageous steps to change their own lives for the better. And each of them has gone even further, reaching out to help improve the lives of those around them. All three of them have dedicated themselves to sharing the gift of reading.

Maria, Daisy, and Julia are just three of the hundreds of thousands of people in this country whose lives have been affected by poor reading skills. A surprisingly large number of Americans are what is often called "functionally illiterate." That is, they cannot read or write well enough to get along, or function, very well in today's society. They might not be able to figure out the right dosage to take from a bottle of medicine, or completely fill out a job application, or find an intersection on a map. Statistics about literacy in America reveal some sad facts. Three out of four people receiving food stamps have very poor reading skills. Forty-three percent of the adults considered functionally illiterate live below the poverty line. And seven out of ten prison inmates are functionally illiterate. These are the realities Julia Burney was thinking about when she said, "I knew from the time I was a little girl that reading was power. . . . You *cannot* thrive in this society without reading well. I arrest people who are unable to read their rights, and I think how hopeless life must look for them."

The three women whose stories appear here once faced odds that must have seemed hopeless. But instead of giving up, they took responsibility for turning their lives around. Maria Cárdenas, Daisy Russell, and Julia Burney each recognized the power that reading provides, and each has claimed that power for her own.

Maria Cárdenas

An orange marigold planted in a tin cup isn't much. It's just a spot of color, a touch of beauty. But to Maria Cárdenas, the marigold was precious.

To understand why, you must know something about Maria's life.

Maria was born in Mexico, the second oldest of what were eventually eight children. When she was four, she went to live with an aunt and uncle. Her mother and father had left Mexico to become migrant workers in the United States. They had paid someone eight hundred dollars to smuggle them across the border. When Maria was seven, her parents sent for the children to join them in Texas.

Migrant workers can't afford much of a childhood. Within a short time, little Maria was working in the fields. Her days were filled with backbreaking labor, hunger, bug bites, sickness, drunken men cursing and fighting, hands stained with tomato oils, scary snakes hiding among the crops, and constant travel. She picked citrus fruit and cucumbers in Florida, potatoes in Tennessee, peppers in North Carolina, and tomatoes in Ohio and Indiana. The family moved wherever the crops were ready.

Their home was a room in whatever migrant camp they were staying in. The word "home" is usually a warm, comforting one. But these rooms weren't warm or comforting. They were very bare, just four walls, furnished with a two-burner gas stove that flared up in scary, unexpected ways. If the family was lucky, there were mattresses on the floor.

Everything else was outside. The workers washed their dishes outside, under a hose. Toilets were holes in the ground, surrounded by flimsy

Maria enjoys working in the garden she's created behind her home.

walls. Cold showers were outside as well. Nowhere that Maria looked was there anything to feed her hungry mind and heart.

So the marigold was important. The spring that

Maria was ten, she went with her mother to a flea market. Someone there was selling plants. Somehow she begged enough change from her mother to buy just one of the seedlings. Planted tenderly in an empty soup can, the flower was the only thing that Maria owned. Even the clothes on her back were shared among several sisters, but the marigold was hers.

She carried it during the long car trips and watered it faithfully. As the family reached each new camp, she placed it in a sunny spot. The little plant traveled with her for an entire season, from Florida to Tennessee and on to Ohio. She treasured it until one night when her father and his friends were drunk and somebody kicked it to pieces.

That was typical of her father. Maria was sad, but she knew better than to complain. Depending on his mood, he would have either laughed at her or beaten her. When Maria had first arrived in the United States, her father seemed concerned for his children. He enrolled them in school, made sure they had supplies of crayons and paper, and bragged to his friends that they were going to become educated. He needed them to learn English so that they could translate his words to the grocer, the doctor, the police officer.

But something happened to him as the years went on. His drinking grew heavier and heavier. His occasional slaps at his wife turned into frequent, terrible beatings. Soon he was hitting his children as well. He stopped working altogether and spent his days sitting by the fields, drinking beer, watching his family work. The kids didn't pick fast enough to suit him, so he threw stones and vegetables at them and called them names. At the week's end, he collected everyone's pay.

All the workers knew about him. "In a migrant camp, like everywhere, you have an upper class and a lower class," Maria says. "If your father was the crew leader—the boss man—you were the rich kids.

You had new clothes. Sometimes you even got to go to the movies. If your dad was an OK guy who worked hard, you were in the middle class. But if your dad was the camp drunk, you were the bottom of the barrel. That was us: the trash of the trash. The crew leader's kids wouldn't even speak to us. When we ended up in the same schools, they pretended they didn't know us."

Because of the family's traveling, Maria had never gone to school very steadily. She would be enrolled now and then, here and there, for a few weeks at a time. As her father grew more brutal, she attended even less. When picking was heavy, she had to stay home to work. If the younger children got sick, Maria was expected to care for them. In the camps she heard only Spanish, so her English skills weren't very good. As a result, she fell further and further behind in her studies.

"I don't know how I got through elementary school, much less to high school," Maria says. "I only knew how to add, subtract, and multiply. I could read enough to help my mother fill out forms in English, but not much more than that." She didn't ask for help. Her hard life had made Maria very shy and quiet. She did what she was told, speaking only in a whisper. At school, she was like a silent ghost sitting in the back of the room. "When the teacher told the class, 'Read this book and write a report,' I just didn't do it," she says. "I knew she wasn't talking to me."

Maria's family smiles for the camera. From left are Jasmine, Korak, Maria, and Alfonso.

Finally, when she was 13, something happened to change the course of Maria's life. Her mother ran away after two weeks of terrible beatings. She had warned the children that she might. When Maria went to school the next day, she told a counselor what had happened. The counselor called the police, and Maria's father was arrested and put in jail. He never lived with the family again, although he continued to harass them. Sometimes he would stand outside their house and yell at his wife, "You're gonna be a prostitute. Those kids are gonna be no-good drug addicts and criminals. They're gonna end up in jail."

As shy and quiet as Maria was, her father's words still enraged her. Somehow, a desire for learning and a better life was alive within her. She dreamed of getting an education, of wearing pretty clothes, of doing work that people respected. She didn't know how she would ever achieve her dreams, but she didn't let them die.

Now that her father was gone, the family was not traveling so much anymore. Maria was able to stay in one school for a while. To her amazement, a teacher, Mrs. Mercer, began to pay special attention to her. Mrs. Mercer seemed to like Maria and thought she was smart. She offered Maria a job in the Western clothing store she and her husband owned. Every Saturday Maria worked at the store, helping to translate for Spanish-speaking customers. She was paid twenty dollars. Proudly, she presented this money to her mother. "I thought, 'I can actually do more than field work!'" she says today. That thought made her dreams seem a little closer to reality.

Maria worked at the store for two years. The month of her sixteenth birthday, Mrs. Mercer recommended her for a job in a local supermarket. Six weeks later, the manager told her he was promoting her to head cashier. Maria was beside herself with happiness. Surely, she thought, her luck had truly changed. She had a good job. She no longer lived in fear of her father's beatings. She was on the way to becoming her school's first Spanish-speaking graduate.

But Maria was about to meet an even more heartbreaking challenge.

The same night that he told her about the promotion, Maria's manager offered to let her off early, so that she could come in early in the morning to open the store. She was delighted. She couldn't wait to tell everyone her wonderful news. But she had no way to get home. Her brother would not pick her up until eleven. Then, to her relief, someone she knew came into the store. He was a friend of her brother's, someone Maria had worked with in the fields. When he offered her a lift home, she gratefully accepted.

She never made it home. She didn't make it to her new promotion, either. Instead of taking her home, the man attacked Maria and raped her.

At Florida Gulf Coast University, Maria discusses techniques for teaching reading with one of her instructors, Dr. Charleen Olliff.

In the course of one awful night, Maria's hopeful visions of the future were snuffed out, seemingly forever. She had been kidnapped, beaten, and raped. But according to the rules of her old-fashioned Mexican society, none of that mattered. She had done a shameful thing; she was disgraced. Her attacker had just been acting like a man. It was her fault for being alone with him. She must have done something to encourage him.

When Maria learned she was pregnant, she saw only one path open to her. She married her rapist, dropped out of tenth grade, and moved with him to Oklahoma.

In her marriage, Maria found herself walking down the same road her mother had walked before her. Her new husband drank heavily and beat Maria mercilessly. When her daughter, Antonietta, was born, Maria took comfort in loving someone and being loved in return. But she felt sad about bringing her daughter up in the midst of fear and violence.

A brother of Maria's, Joel, happened to be living in the same Oklahoma town. When he saw Maria, he also saw the bruises her husband had given her. Unlike others, Joel did not stay silent. He did not say what had happened was Maria's fault. He encouraged her to leave her husband. "Go on; you can make it," he told her.

"I can't," Maria would protest. She was embarrassed to go home. She knew people would criticize her for "failing" as a wife.

But Joel wouldn't give up. "I'm going to tell Mother what is going on. I'll make her understand." Joel did talk to their mother. He insisted that Maria was not to blame for her situation. He told her Maria was being abused and was going to leave her husband. Their mother accepted what he said. Maria threw her clothes into her car, took her little girl, and left Oklahoma for her mother's home in Florida. Her husband responded the same way her father had years before. "You'll be on food stamps! You can't amount to anything on your own!" he told her. But Maria proved him wrong. Back in Florida, she worked all day in the fields and until midnight at the supermarket. She kept up the payments on her car, didn't go on welfare, and felt happy and proud of herself.

One worry, though, kept pushing itself into her mind. Antonietta was growing up and beginning kindergarten. She did well there. Maria loved it when Antonietta would come home with her little books, hand them to her mom, and say, "Read to me." But as Maria read the simple books, she kept thinking ahead. Some day, before too long, Antonietta was going to come home with books that were too hard for her to read. What would she think when her mother said, "I can't read it"? Maria wondered. And what would Maria think of herself?

Maria had heard there were programs that taught adults to read. But in some ways, she was still as scared and shy as she had been as a little girl.

Maria shows her sister, Jane Ireland, literature from the hospital that explains how a liver transplant works.

She didn't dare go to anyone and ask for help. So she decided to do it on her own.

"Teaching myself to read became the most important goal in my life," she says. She began with Antonietta's kindergarten books. Sometimes she thought how silly she must look: a grown woman struggling to read *The Cat in the Hat*. But no one was watching, so she kept trying. At night, after Antonietta was asleep, Maria read everything she could find. She read advertisements that came in the mail. She read cereal boxes. She read the labels on products. Slowly, her skills improved. The day came when she felt ready to try a real, grown-up story. But there was nothing like that in the house.

They lived near a library. Again and again, Antonietta had asked her mother to take her there. Again and again, Maria had said no. She felt too scared, too threatened. What would the library be like? What if someone asked her what she was doing there? Was she even allowed to go in? How would she know the rules? Finally, summoning all her courage, she walked inside with Antonietta.

It didn't work. In her panic, the library seemed just as scary as she had imagined. She felt lost among all the people walking quickly around, knowing what they were doing. She didn't have a clue where to begin to look for a book. Hardly able to breathe, she grabbed Antonietta's hand and dragged her out again. Ashamed, yet relieved to be out of there, she told Antonietta to use the library at her school.

Maria continued to struggle on alone. Finally, she was ready to take her GED exam. She passed. Years after she thought she had lost her chance forever, Maria was a high-school graduate. Slowly, she was beginning to achieve at least small pieces of her dream.

One thing that had no place in that dream, Maria was certain, was a man. Her experience with her father and her ex-husband had convinced her of that. The supermarket where she worked was a popular place among migrant workers. Because of their constant travel, few migrants have checking accounts. As a result, on Friday night and Saturday, the store would be full of workers paying a fee to cash their paychecks. Sometimes they tried to chat up the pretty cashier. Maria wouldn't give them the time of day. All she wanted to do was take care of her daughter, pay her bills, and keep learning.

But there was one fellow who just wouldn't go away. His name was Alfonso Cárdenas. Maria noticed he came through her checkout line again and again. He would drop into the store on any excuse, if only to buy a pack of gum. Other times he would stop in after his martial-arts class for a bottle of water. Unlike the other men, he didn't make obnoxious comments to the girls. He seemed very shy, only saying "hi" or "how are you today?"

One evening, Maria was especially tired. It had been a hard day, and she had to close up the supermarket at 11, meaning her day would be even longer than usual. "And along comes this guy," she says today, with a laugh. "He says, 'Could I talk to you after you get off?' And I had no patience with this. I said, 'No you can't! We have nothing to talk about!' Believe me, I was not nice."

But he came back again, still asking. "I told him 'No, no, no, no, I am not interested. I have no time. I'm too busy. I have a little girl. I don't want

Maria, her sister Jane (left), and her daughter Antonietta (center) share a joke as they walk around Maria's neighborhood.

anything to do with a man.' But to myself I had to admit that he seemed nice."

Finally, a girlfriend invited Maria to go with her and her husband to a flea market one Saturday. "And when they picked me up, guess who was along?" Maria said. She gave up and spent the afternoon walking around the market with Alfonso. The next time he came into the store, he invited her to the beach. "I said no, I have my little girl, I want to spend my time off with her." And he said, "Bring her along!"

Over the next months, Maria learned more about Alfonso. He too was from Mexico, from a remote village without an elementary school or even electricity or running water. At the age of 18, without speaking a word of English, he had crossed the border and begun following the harvest. She learned he was a hard worker; a steady, quiet man; and that he didn't drink. He told her he admired what she had accomplished, that he respected her thirst for education. She watched him play gently with Antonietta. Slowly she came to believe that this was a man she could trust, and she and Alfonso were married. Together, they worked in the fields, but close to home so that Antonietta could stay in the same school. When the picking season ended, they both found local work.

In 1987, their son, Korak, was born. That same

*Every day, Maria has to take a variety of medications to keep her
damaged liver working until a new organ becomes available.*

year, Maria was working for Redlands Christian
Migrant Association, an organization that provides
services to migrant children. One day in the office,
she noticed a book that made her heart jump. It was
a collection of stories about migrant workers called

Dark Harvest. In those years since her failed visit to the library, Maria had still never read an entire book. But as she leafed through this one, she realized that she read well enough to understand it all. Better than that, these stories were about people like her. With growing fascination she read it cover to cover. She learned about other migrant workers who, like her, had earned their GEDs. And even more exciting—some of them had gone on to college. Some of them were now teachers. Their stories made Maria realize that her dream wasn't impossible at all.

Alfonso learned about a federal program that helped seasonal farm workers go to college. Maria applied to the program and was accepted. Her placement tests showed that her reading, English, and math skills were at the seventh-grade level. She was encouraged; she had feared they would be lower. The program recruiter suggested that Maria enroll in some Adult Basic Education classes to raise her scores. Eagerly, Maria agreed. She loved the classes, and before very long, her scores were above the twelfth-grade level.

By 1994, Maria and Alfonso's family had grown to include Jasmine. It was that fall that Maria Cárdenas—migrant child, teenage mother, high-school dropout, and victim of abuse—became a freshman at Edison Community College in Fort Myers, Florida. From her first days as a college student, Maria found success. Her grades were outstanding. She was honored with membership in Phi Theta Kappa, the national honor society for junior colleges, and the International Key Club.

After graduating from Edison, Maria moved on to enroll at Florida Gulf Coast University, where she is now a senior. Her degree in elementary education will allow her to teach other migrant children, encouraging them to dream their own dreams and make them a reality.

The entire Cárdenas family has embraced

On the back porch of their home, Antonietta plays with her Quaker parrot as Maria looks on.

Maria's love of learning. Alfonso has completed a number of courses to be trained as an air-conditioning technician. He has also enrolled in classes to earn his own GED. Antonietta will graduate with honors this year from the same university her mother attends. She plans to attend law school. Korak and Jasmine are good students who love to read. They joke that the library is their "second home," and it's Maria that they have to finally drag home. The family owns a pretty house in Fort Myers surrounded by the flowers, trees, and shrubs that Maria loves to grow.

Maria is proud of her family and grateful for the support that they have shown her. "Sometimes I doubt myself," she admits. "I've lived in two such different worlds." There are people who criticize Maria's decision to go to school, to plan for a career, to have a life outside her home and family. "For them, being a good woman means staying home, making fresh *tortillas* every day, watching the *telenovelas* (Spanish-language soap operas), and having a thousand kids," she says. "Maybe I'm self-ish, but I think life has more to offer me than that."

After all that Maria has been through, it seems almost too cruel that today she is facing a crisis in her own health. But that is the case. In the fall of 2001, she had major surgery. After she returned home from the hospital, she began to notice some frightening symptoms. Her legs and belly swelled up. She felt sick all the time. When she called the doctor, she was told that the symptoms were just side effects of the pain medication she was taking.

But several days later, after Alfonso had left for work and the children were in school, Maria became very sick. To her terror, she began vomiting blood. She called Alfonso, who rushed her to the local emergency room. There she heard a doctor say he would have to put her to sleep and put a tube down her throat to find the source of the blood. That was Tuesday morning. She didn't remember anything else until Friday.

"Another doctor came into my room. He was very gentle," she says. "He sat down and told me that I had a disease called cirrhosis, and that it had destroyed my liver. I said, 'Can you fix it?' He said no, that my only hope would be a liver transplant."

The doctor explained that the cirrhosis was the

result of another disease, Hepatitis C. Years before, when Maria had no insurance, she had sometimes gone to a public health clinic. At one point, a worker told her she had Hepatitis C, but never explained what that meant or what Maria should do about it. She didn't feel sick, so she assumed the disease wasn't something to worry about. "At a place like that, nobody tells you anything," she says. "They have no time for you. You're poor; you're dirt; you're nothing." In fact, as soon as she was diagnosed with Hepatitis C, Maria should have started taking medicine to protect her liver. She should have been examined regularly to catch the damage before it was too severe. Now she was very seriously ill.

At this time, Maria is a patient in the liver-transplant program at Shands Hospital in Gainesville, Florida. She is on a nationwide waiting list for a new liver. People on that list receive livers as other people who have volunteered to be organ donors die. The predicted waiting time for a transplant is three years. As doctors try to keep Maria healthy enough to handle the wait, she is frequently at their offices or in the hospital.

In the meantime, in and around medical appointments, Maria continues going to college. She has recently begun her student teaching in an elementary school. "It's a dream come true for me," she said. "To be back in the classroom, not as a scared little kid but as a teacher—who would have thought it was possible?" But it is true. Maria—the scared, silent child in the back of the classroom; the young mother who worried that she could not understand her own little girl's books—is teaching these children to read.

Maria Cárdenas has traveled a long way from her earliest days in the migrant fields. As a child, she had to find beauty and hope in the simplest things—for instance, an orange marigold in a tin cup. Today, in spite of her worries about her health, she sees reasons for rejoicing all around her. Her family, her home, her marriage, and her success in school are all sources of great happiness. "Learning to read was the beginning of so many beautiful things for me," she says. "I've had a wonderful, wonderful life."

Daisy Russell

Scared.   Lonely.   Ashamed.

These are the words that come to mind when Daisy Russell remembers going to school.

"Back then, teachers were always making us stand in lines and giving us words to spell," Daisy remembers. "It was like a spelling bee. I always went down on my very first word. Even if it were a simple word like 'also,' I would get it wrong and have to sit down. Everyone would laugh."

The failure and the mocking laughter stayed the same. The school didn't. Between first and sixth grades, Daisy attended seventeen different schools.

It wasn't Daisy's choice to change schools so often. She, along with her mother, was at the mercy of her restless father. "He moved us all over the country looking for the pot of gold at the end of the rainbow," Daisy says. "I don't think he ever found it." More than once, Daisy walked out of school at the day's end to find her parents waiting for her, their car packed with everything they owned. With no warning, they were moving again.

"When Mother would tell Dad that we needed to stay in one place so I could catch up in school, he would laugh and ask, 'Why?'" Daisy says. "Then he'd answer himself: 'Girls don't need an education.'"

Daisy's father had not wanted a daughter. He considered girls "worthless" for anything but keeping house and having babies. He valued Daisy so little that when she was about a year old, he tried to give her away.

Her mother was at work, and her father was sup-

Daisy Russell

Daisy's dog, Happy, sits on his mistress's lap while he poses for the camera.

posed to be caring for her. By chance, her mother got off work a bit early. When she arrived home, she met a strange man and woman leaving her house. The woman had little Daisy in her arms.

"What are you doing with my baby?" her mother asked. The woman looked shocked. "*Your* baby?" she said. Bit by bit, the story came out. The couple could not have a child of their own. Daisy's father had told them that his wife had died, and he had offered to let them adopt the baby. "I never knew what Dad had planned to tell my mother when she found me gone," Daisy says, "but I'm sure it wouldn't have been the truth."

As Daisy grew older, her father's feelings about her did not change. To make things worse, he was a heavy drinker, he had a bad temper, and he had been abused by his own parents. Put together, those facts had terrible results for his daughter.

Daisy's childhood was marked by black eyes, bruised ribs, and brutal kicks from feet wearing heavy work boots. There were times her mouth was so cut and swollen from the blows of her father's fists that she could not eat solid food. When Daisy's mother tried to protect her, the beating would fall on her instead.

"He'd been beaten growing up himself," Daisy says. "I think he had no idea there were ways to deal with his anger other than hitting."

The family's constant moves served to protect Daisy's father. When Daisy would go to school covered with cuts and bruises, she would tell her teacher she had fallen, or walked into a doorway. She was too frightened of her father to tell the truth. By the time the teacher might have become suspicious about her frequent injuries, or concerned about her struggles to learn, the family had left town. There was no one to come to her aid.

And anyway, Daisy had little reason to think an adult might help her. Life had taught her that adults would not protect her. Not only did her father beat her, but since she had been just a toddler, an uncle had been sexually abusing her. Once again, a grownup in her life had betrayed her trust, and once again, there was no one to turn to for help.

As Daisy sees it, her painful, rootless life could have had different effects. Under similar circumstances, another child might have become aggressive, openly angry; the kind of child who is constantly "acting out." Another child might become outgoing and greedy, trying to snatch anything that came her way. But Daisy just became quieter and quieter. In school, she was too frightened to tell her teachers that she didn't understand the assignments, or much of anything that was going on. Rather than draw attention to how far behind she was, she tried to make herself invisible.

By the time Daisy was ten, she and her mother were living in fear for their lives. Her father was drinking more heavily than ever, and his beatings were becoming increasingly ferocious. After he

When Daisy won a scholarship for a story she wrote about her life, she used the money to buy her first computer. She writes stories and poems on the computer and uses e-mail to keep in touch with friends as well.

sobered up, he would not even remember what he had done. Finally, Daisy's mother took action. She and her little girl ran away, leaving no clue as to where they had gone. Daisy never saw her father again. "I don't know if he's dead or alive, and I don't care to know," she says.

Daisy was finally free of her father's physical abuse. But the beatings had damaged her spirit as much as they had her body, and those unseen effects lingered. She was still the shy, terrified girl at the back of the classroom, her head down, hoping to get through one more day without being noticed. Struggling through one grade after another, she never learned to read much better than a typical second-grader. For her mother, making ends meet was the priority, not helping Daisy learn. "I do remember a couple of parent-teacher conferences, and having the teacher suggest that Mother help me learn by reading the newspaper," she says. "But I'm sure that listening to me spend twenty minutes trying to read one paragraph was pretty boring for my mom. So that never went anywhere."

By the time Daisy was 16 and in the eighth grade, she was eager to get away from the daily humiliation of being "the stupidest kid on the face of the earth." She dropped out.

Daisy was relieved to be done with school. But then a surprising thing happened. Away from the classroom, with no kids to laugh at her and no teacher to lose patience with her, she discovered a desire to tackle her reading problem on her own. "When I was about 18, a lady gave me a copy of *Modern Romance* magazine," she remembers. "I wanted to read the stories in it. I wasn't completely illiterate, and I thought that if I tried hard enough, I could do it. But reading that magazine took me *months*. There were so many words I didn't know. If Mom was there, I'd holler at her and spell the word and say, 'What is that?' If she wasn't around, I'd try to use the dictionary."

One way or another, Daisy struggled through that issue of *Modern Romance*. That taste of success made her want more. She had figured out a few tricks on her own. "Even if I couldn't understand all of a dictionary definition, sometimes I could get enough out if it to figure out the word. And I learned that I could often skip a word and figure out from what came *after* it what it might mean."

Daisy's job as a school custodian gave her a chance for more reading practice. At night, cleaning the elementary classrooms, she found shelves of easy-to-read books. There was no one around to laugh at her, so she took the opportunity. She began by picking up a cartoon book, *Marmaduke*, which told the adventures of a giant Great Dane. The cartoons were funny and the captions were short and not too difficult. On her nightly breaks, Daisy would sit in the empty classroom and read *Marmaduke*. "I read the whole thing through, without any help," she recalls proudly.

As reading became slightly easier for her, Daisy found a type of book that excited her—science fiction. "Not the gory stuff about aliens eating people!" she says. "But books from the *Star Trek* series—I really liked them."

Clearly, Daisy had come a long way. But her progress was slow, and there were still many words that she did not understand. And personally, Daisy

Ar the public library, Daisy shares a book with her granddaughter Tiffany. "My grandma helped me learn to read," Tiffany says.

was still very shy and withdrawn.

"Oh, back then, you would have been lucky if you'd gotten 'Good morning' out of me," she says. "There was such a wall around me." It was a wall of anger and hurt, grown out of the abuse she had suffered. It was also a wall of embarrassment. Daisy desperately wanted to read better. But she could not imagine, as a grown woman, admitting that to anyone.

But on December 5, 1979, Daisy took a job that would change her life forever. She went to work in the Bendix Aerospace factory in Kansas City, Missouri. (The company has since changed its name to Honeywell.) There she heard about in-company programs designed to help employees complete their education. One of them was an adult literacy program, staffed by tutors trained in the Laubach Literacy methods. (The Laubach program is named after its founder, Frank Laubach.) Daisy stubbornly resisted asking for help. She worked at her job for ten years, aware that some of her fellow employees were improving their reading skills, before she took the step herself.

It was an encounter at a party that changed her

mind. "A friend of mine was a student in the reading program," she recalls. "In 1989, he was graduating from Book 1 to Book 2. His tutor had a little get-together to celebrate, and she invited me." At the party, Daisy got into conversation with Verna Cooper, the head of the company's education program. Verna seemed kind and sympathetic, and Daisy found the courage to confide in her. "I told her that I wanted to finish my education, but that I didn't read and write well enough to do that," Daisy says. "She said, 'Let's fix you up with a tutor.'"

Daisy was paired with Earl Riggs, an engineer trained as a Laubach reading tutor. For the next eighteen months, the two met for an hour, twice a week, on company time. Together, they worked to give Daisy the tools she had not been able to develop on her own.

"The key to my learning to read was phonics. That was something I had no idea of," she says.

Daisy gives her grandson Bradley a boost on the playground.
Daisy enjoys giving her grandchildren the kind of positive
experiences she never had as a child.

Phonics involves "sounding out" letters and sylla-
bles. "When I was reading on my own, and I came
across a word I didn't recognize, I had no way to
decipher it," Daisy explains. "With Earl sitting there
beside me, I learned how to break a word into its
parts."

To her surprise, working with a tutor turned out
to be a lot of fun. "We kidded around all the time,"
Daisy says. "For instance, I remember when I first
hit the word 'people.' With its silent 'o' there in the
middle, I could not figure that word out. When
Earl finally told me what it said, I studied it and
said, 'That doesn't say 'people.' It says 'PEE
OPLE.' So ever after that, when the word would
come up in our lessons, we'd say 'Pee Ople' and get
to laughing so hard that the director would come
over and say, 'If you two don't quiet down, you're
going to have to leave!'"

Once Daisy began to develop the tools she
needed, her progress was rapid. And as her reading

ability grew, so did her self-confidence. When her company offered an in-house math program, Daisy jumped at the chance to enroll. She discovered that she not only could do math, but that she loved it. In the fall of 1991, the eighth-grade dropout enrolled in a college algebra class.

She got an A.

"I'd never gotten an A in *anything*," Daisy says. "I thought, well, if I did that, maybe it's time to try for the GED." Her employer offered a program to prepare people for the General Equivalency Degree examination, and Daisy enrolled. After six months, her tutor said she was ready to take the exam.

A month after taking the exam, on September 6, 1992, Daisy came home from work to find an envelope waiting. Inside was her GED diploma. At the age of 44, Daisy Russell was a high-school graduate.

Much has happened in Daisy's life since that day. The scared, silent little girl has become an outspoken champion of adult literacy. She has given a workshop

Daisy Russell

When Michael Pickens was in elementary school. Daisy tutored him in reading. Since then, he's been "a member of the family," says Daisy. Tiffany says, "He's like my big brother!"

at the national Laubach Literacy convention. She speaks before church gatherings, Rotary meetings, and any other group that invites her to tell about her experience. She has appeared on local television shows and radio programs. Most importantly of all, Daisy herself has become a Laubach tutor.

"I talk to *anyone* about being a new reader," Daisy says. "I talk to strangers on the street, at the mall, at the beauty shop, anywhere I am. I hand out cards with the numbers for the local Laubach centers in and around Kansas City. I want everybody to know that if they have trouble reading or writing, or know someone who does, that there is help available. They have nothing to be ashamed of. The people who need to hang their heads in shame are the adults who had control over their lives as children."

As she looks back on her remarkable journey, Daisy gives special credit to two people: her husband Don, and Peggy Otten, the former reading-program coordinator at Honeywell.

"Don has been my biggest fan and supporter," Daisy says fondly. "This is Don in a nutshell: Once I was working and working with a math problem, and I was tired out and just could not get it for the life of me. I finally picked up that book and threw it across the room and said 'That's it! I'm too stupid; I can't do this.' And Don just quietly picked up the book and said, 'C'mon, honey, let's go for a drive.'

Daisy looks through her "brag book," in which she keeps papers and pictures that remind her of special accomplishments. The eagle on the front of the book reminds her to fly high!

We went out and got some ice cream, and I relaxed, and by the time I got back, I was ready to face that problem again. I was just plain tired out, and he knew just what I needed."

About Peg Otten, Daisy says, "She gave me the gumption to start learning to read. I did a lot of what I did because she asked me to. She was the first person who told me, 'You *are* smart! You *can* do this!'" Even today, Daisy cannot speak without tears about what that kind of encouragement meant to her. Her voice is hoarse with emotion as she adds, "You tell a child she's stupid and worthless often enough, she eventually believes you. She quits trying. But Peggy—she made me believe maybe that wasn't true."

Today, Daisy is in yet another phase of her life. Back surgery two years ago left her with metal rods and screws in her backbone, and she is no longer able to do the physical work required of her at Honeywell. She has retired and spends much of her time caring for her grandchildren, eight-year-old Tiffany and two-year-old Bradley. "My grand-babies," she says, "are my number one priority." Having had such a painful childhood herself, she is clearly determined that her grandchildren will grow up differently. "Until I was a teenager, I didn't know that all daddies didn't beat their kids," she

Daisy with the men in her life: Shorty Dunn, on the left, is a neighbor and "the good dad I never had." Daisy holds grandson Bradley. On the right is her husband, Don, who Daisy calls "my rock."

says, adding firmly, "There is no hitting in this house."

But it's clear that, having tasted what life has to offer, Daisy will not be content staying home for long. "I haven't taken a college class for two years, and I don't have a reading student right now," she says. "Retirement is driving me nuts! I can only do so much housework, and I've read every book I own, most of them twice. So I'm thinking about taking an evening course soon, probably in creative writing."

Public speaking, college courses, creative writing, tutoring, TV appearances—this frightened, illiterate, "worthless" girl has traveled far. In looking back on the cycle of abuse that ran through her family, and the reading problems that it created for her, Daisy feels satisfaction at what she has accomplished. "It wasn't right that any of those things happened to me," she says today. "But it would have been just as wrong for me to pass them on. If I don't break the cycle, who will?"

Julia Burney

Julia Burney was afraid of many things as a child. Mostly, she was afraid of Fridays.

Fridays were the days her parents headed out to the bars. Julia would go to bed but lie awake for hours, too tense to sleep. Eventually her mother and father would return home, and then the brawling would begin.

Voices would grow louder. Crashes would echo through the apartment. There would be the sound of blows and cries.

"Call the police!" her mother would often scream. "He's killing me!"

Julia keeps this photograph of herself in a ragged dress to remind herself of the poverty she grew up in. She is shown with her younger sister, and her mother and father, who were 13 and 17 when she was born.

"You call the cops and I'll beat you too!" her father would shout.

"Julia Mae, do something!" the younger children would shriek.

And eight-year-old Julia, the oldest of what were eventually twelve siblings (two died in infancy), would try to dodge her father's fist to reach the phone. If she made it, and if the phone hadn't been disconnected, she would dial the number of the police department.

And then, she remembers, it was as if a miracle happened.

"The moment the officers appeared, everything changed. My dad would sit up, listen to them, and act right. My home would be peaceful again.

"So that became my dream," Julia says today. "Someday, I would do that for another child."

Julia would achieve her dream. But she had a lot to go through first.

Julia lived in Racine, Wisconsin. She had been born in Mississippi, but her parents had moved up

North to look for better jobs when Julia was three. Her parents were hardly more than children themselves; when Julia was born, her mother was 13 and her father 17. Neither had finished junior high school. Neither could read or write well.

Their daughter's memories of them are bittersweet.

"They were hard-working people, well-respected in Racine," she says. "They were generous—they taught us to share whatever we had, and to look down on no one. They had plenty of common sense, what my father called 'motherwit.' As we were growing up, he'd say, 'You might have more schooling than I do, but I have motherwit.' And he did.

"But they were so young when they had us, and there were so many of us," she goes on. "Imagine all those mouths to feed and bills to pay! I am amazed that they accomplished what they did. They raised us and kept us together. With all they had to cope with, I can understand why they drank. But alcohol ruined a large portion of our lives. I loved my parents, but I hated their drinking."

As the oldest of so many children, Julia was expected to take on a great deal of responsibility. There wasn't much time for her to be a child. "I remember playing outside with friends, but those memories are fleeting," she says. "After just a few minutes, it was, 'Julia Mae, get in here and start dinner.'"

The family's poverty was crushing. The electricity was turned off so many times that Julia says today, "I grew up in the dark." Nowadays in Racine, where the winter wind chill can plunge to 60 below zero, public utilities are forbidden to turn off people's heat for non-payment of bills until April 15. That was not the case when Julia was a child. During many frigid Wisconsin winters, her family tried to warm itself with space heaters, candles, and extra layers of clothing.

Compared with the poverty and occasional violence of her home, school was a welcome refuge for Julia. "I loved school from day one," she says. Her first reading books introduced her to Dick, Jane, and Spot, and to a lifelong love affair with books. "Reading came naturally to me," she says. "But any encouragement to read stopped at our front door." Her parents were supportive of their children's attending school. But the idea of reading for pleasure was so foreign to them that they did not understand it in Julia.

In addition, there was the problem of money. "To my parents, a book might as well have cost a million dollars," Julia explains. "If I did bring home a school book, they were afraid I'd lose it or damage it. So up it would go on top of the refrigerator, where it would be safe."

But Julia found a place where she could read to her heart's content. That place was her Aunt Ruby's house, where she would often go to babysit. Aunt

"Tell the kids I love them"
- *GOD*

The photograph on the wall above Julia shows her in her police officer's uniform, distributing books to children on the streets of Racine.

Ruby had many books, as well as magazines like *True Stories* that Julia read to learn about "love and life and romance—stuff my parents didn't talk about." Aunt Ruby encouraged Julia to read and to talk about what she was reading.

Julia says today, "I learned to read at school. I learned to *love* reading at Aunt Ruby's."

Julia's love of reading helped her become a fine student, one determined to prepare for a better future. "Peer pressure" had no meaning for her; she simply ignored anyone who suggested she should not care about her schooling. And drink and drugs did not attract her at all. "In their way, my parents taught me a great lesson," she says. "You know how most kids at least try cigarettes? Not me. I have never smoked even one cigarette. Never tasted alcohol. Never used an ounce of marijuana. I looked at my parents' example and thought, 'That's what I'd become.'"

But Julia had her own kind of weakness. Her parents had never been ones to show affection. "They never said, 'I love you.' They never hugged or kissed us. To them, putting a roof over our heads and food on the table was love. But I wanted some-one to *tell* me." When Julia was 17, a boy came along. He told Julia, "I love you." She soon found herself pregnant with her first child.

"I confused sex with love," Julia says today. "And eventually, I was raising four kids on my own."

Julia Burney

Adjusting to motherhood was not as difficult for Julia as it might have been for another teenager. "I'd been taking care of babies since I was one myself," she says. "When I was nine years old, I was

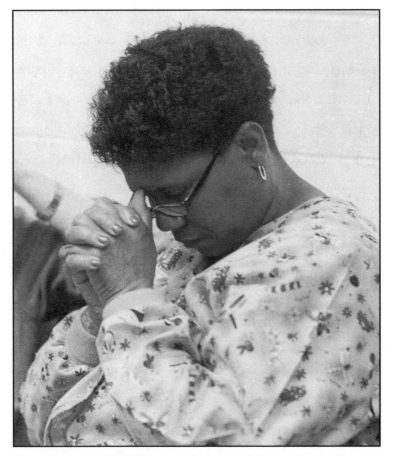

A quiet moment. During her busy days, Julia often bows her head to say a quick prayer.

67

giving children baths, fixing their hair, making meals and calling the gas company to get an extension on the bill. So having my own baby was not such a change. What was hard was making ends meet." When her first child was born, Julia transferred to a school that offered night classes in order to earn her high school diploma. She started working, usually two jobs at once, to support her children. On her eighteenth birthday, she moved out of her parents' house and into her own apartment.

As the years went on, Julia worked as a restaurant chef—drawing on her years of experience cooking for her family—and then as a teacher's assistant. In 1979, she was hired as a clerk by the Racine police department. Five years later, she fulfilled her early dream of becoming a police officer. Not surprisingly, she quickly proved herself to be outstanding at dealing what she calls "civil disturbances"— calls to homes where fighting was going on.

"I'd go into those homes, and I'd know there

were children hiding in the bedrooms, scared to death," Julia says. "I'd get backup and go into those bedrooms and sit with the children, hugging them, promising them that things would be better, telling them they didn't have to live like this forever. Every time I comforted a child like that, it was like comforting a piece of myself."

And when Julia went into those homes, she noticed something that many other officers might have missed: If there were any books in the house at all, they were on top of the refrigerator.

The sight tore at her heart. Memories would flood back to her when she saw those books, kept high out of reach. She knew what the children in those homes were being denied: not only books, but the hopes and dreams that books could inspire.

"I knew from the time I was a little girl that reading was power," she says. "My parents were crippled by their inability to read well. You *cannot* thrive in this society without reading well. I arrest people who are unable to read their rights, and I think how hopeless life must look for them."

Julia herself not only enjoys reading, but her love of books has benefited her professionally. She speaks beautifully, with a large vocabulary at her command. At the police station, she was frequently complimented on her clearly-written arrest reports. "I write well because I read," she says. "If you read, you learn to write. You absorb the style, you learn good grammar, you learn to talk properly. Using language well becomes second nature."

Remembering all these things, and thinking of the children growing up knowing nothing of the magic of books, a vision came to Julia. She wanted to do for these children what her Aunt Ruby had done for her. "I wanted to tell them, 'It's okay to read. It's okay to borrow books. You just need to learn to take care of them.' I knew I had to get books into these children's hands. But I didn't know where the books were going to come from."

*Julia and her coworkers sort through a box of books
donated to the Cops 'n Kids Reading Center.*

She adds, "But then I went on a burglary call and God gave them to me."

It was on a night in 1997 that Julia responded to a false alarm at a Racine warehouse. When the warehouse owner unlocked the door to let the officers in, Julia saw a beautiful sight: boxes and boxes of children's books. The books had slight imperfections, so they were going to be shredded and recycled. Julia asked for the books, and the warehouse owner agreed to let her have them.

Julia and some of her fellow officers began hauling the books around in the trunks of their squad cars. When they had any contact with children, the books would come out. They gave books away during school visits, when children would come to the police station, even during traffic stops. At Christmas, a merchant provided a storefront, and the officers hosted a book giveaway. Children came to it pulling wagons and carrying bags to take their precious books home.

For Julia and the other officers, it was a good feeling to see the children's faces light up when they saw an officer in uniform. "I knew how inner-city people regarded the police," Julia remembers. "They didn't have a good flavor in their mouths about us. Throughout my career, my goal was to make people see that there was a human being behind the badge. I wanted them to know that, yeah, I'll arrest you if I have to, but what I *want* to do is keep the peace and make our community a better place to be."

Make no mistake—Julia was never a "soft cop." She won her share of law-enforcement awards for doing what had to be done. But she also gained the reputation of being "the mother of the police force."

She was—and is—a famous hugger. If she spotted a young drug dealer on the street, but didn't see him selling, something like this might occur. She would approach him like the mother and grandmother she is. "I'd say, 'Hey, honey. How you doing? You remember me? I know your momma. Come here, let me give you a hug.'" Taken off guard by this uniformed officer's approach, the young man would hug her back. Holding him tightly in her arms, Julia would murmur, "Sweetheart, you know where this is going to lead you, don't you?" And he would answer, "Yes, ma'am." A woman of faith, Julia would hope that

God would plant a seed in that young man's heart that would grow into something positive. If not, at least Julia would know that she'd tried.

"Maybe I'd see that young man again, dying on the street. Maybe I'd be the one to hear his last words," Julia says. "If I had to be tough, I was tough. But I always tried to treat people the way I'd want an officer to treat my own child."

After the Christmas book giveaway, the Cops 'n Kids program began to take on a life of its own. The local newspaper, the *Journal-Times*, did a story about Julia's efforts. In response, individual and community groups called to ask how they could help. Some businesses held drives to collect used books. Others donated money. Individuals volunteered their time to help sort the books. Police officers loaded bags of books into their squad cars every morning. They gave them out in local parks, on patrol, and on calls. Children who had formerly been afraid of the police began chasing squad cars

Julia Burney

Many volunteer hours have gone into the creation of the Reading Center. The mural behind Julia was painted by two young artists who drove to Wisconsin from Buffalo, NY.

down the street, yelling, "Can I have a book?"

All this was wonderful. But it still wasn't enough for Julia. She wanted a *place* for children to come. She envisioned something like a giant living room: a peaceful, comfortable place where kids could experience the joy of reading.

Julia began searching for a building that could house the place she dreamed of. Then she spotted it—a brick building, smack in the middle of the inner city, which had been boarded up for twenty-eight years. With her usual irresistible energy, she asked a community leader to help her obtain it. The right people were approached, the idea was explained, and the building's owner donated it to Cops 'n Kids.

Meanwhile, the *Journal-Times* article about Cops 'n Kids had been picked up by the Associated Press and reprinted all over the world. In January 1999, Julia received a call from a producer of NBC's *Today* show. *Today* wanted Julia to come to New York to be interviewed by the show's host, Katie Couric. The producer also wanted to send a camera crew to Racine to take pictures of officers handing books out to kids on the streets.

To the producer's astonishment, Julia said no. "I said, thank you very much, but I'm too busy to come to New York. And besides, we don't pass books out on the sidewalk in the middle of the winter in Wisconsin! Do you know how cold it gets here? If you want to do this story, you ought to come here next summer when you can do it right."

The producer tried again. "She said, 'Julia, do you understand—this is the *Today* show? The biggest morning show in the country?"

Julia said she understood. But she still wasn't coming to New York.

So the following July, the *Today* show came to Racine. Katie Couric interviewed Julia and did a touching episode on her efforts to bring books to her community's neediest children.

Julia had great faith in the Cops 'n Kids idea. But what happened next was almost too much for even her to believe.

Producers at the Oprah Winfrey organization saw the *Today* program. They contacted Julia and told her she had been chosen to receive one of Oprah's "Use Your Life" awards. The award carried with it a check for $100,000. In September 2000, Julia appeared on the *Oprah* show to accept the check. During that appearance, she explained more fully what she hoped to do with the center. She described the comfortable furniture; the warm, inviting rooms; the computer lab; and the crafts center that she hoped would eventually be part of the Center.

With the "Use Your Life" money, Julia was able to buy supplies for the renovation of the building. The Racine community came out in force to provide volunteer labor for the job. Many police officers and firefighters contributed their time. Members of the local labor unions worked for free. Businesses and churches raised funds for new windows. High school kids ripped out old drywall and painted. Gradually, the run-down building became a clean, solid home for Cops 'n Kids. There wasn't much *inside* the building but books and some mismatched furniture, but it was a start.

Then in March 2001, Julia got another call from the Oprah organization. The producers wanted her to be on the show again, they said, to update the

When storytime comes, Julia gets into the action along with the children.

audience on the center. Julia was picked up in a limousine and driven the eighty miles to Chicago, where *Oprah* is taped. She was given a room in a hotel and then told that there would be a delay in taping the show—that a man they needed to interview her had missed his flight to Chicago.

For the next three days, Julia waited impatiently in her hotel. She kept getting calls from the producer, saying, "We'll be taping soon—get dressed!" But when she was all ready she'd get another call, saying that another problem had come up and that she would have to wait a little while longer.

Finally the real call came—it was time to tape the show. Julia went to the studio and walked onstage with Oprah. At that point, Oprah confessed that Julia had been told a white lie—in fact, a whole string of them. She wasn't there just to do an update on the program. Instead, during the past three days, an army of people had been very, very busy in Racine. Julia was then invited to look at the Cops 'n Kids Reading Center over a video monitor on stage.

The bare rooms of the center had been filled with comfortable sofas, easy chairs, craft tables, and office furniture donated by the Ethan Allen Company. Beautiful paintings hung on the walls. Thick, colorful rugs covered the floors. Two young artists from Buffalo, New York, had driven ten hours to cover one huge wall with a bright mural. A baby grand piano stood in the auditorium. The

Sears company had donated a complete computer lab. Even the smallest details had been taken care of, down to a basket of warm socks to cover the feet of little readers. Watching the video, Julia sobbed with joy. Many people in the audience shared her happy tears.

The next June, the Cops 'n Kids Reading Center officially opened for business. And today, it is as busy as it is beautiful. Racine's children, from pre-schoolers through eighth-graders, stream through its doors every day. More than 5,000 books are waiting there for the children to read and borrow. Because the books are donated to the center, the children are not fined if they lose or damage one. That doesn't mean, however, that it's okay for the children to be careless with the books. "We talk about the responsibility of keeping the book safe," Julia explains. "We help the children learn to care for books, but without a penalty. In that way, you could think of us as a training library."

But the Center is far more than a library. Besides lending books, it provides many other activities for children. Retired teachers offer tutoring. Children produce works of art in a crafts room, with supplies donated by the local Barnes & Noble store. Plays, concerts, parties, and author's book-signings take place in the center's auditorium. Writing classes encourage children to get their thoughts down on paper. Student teachers from a nearby college come in to help. Doctors and nurses and dentists volunteer their time to check the kids' hearing and vision and teeth. Guest readers come in often, sometimes from local schools. "The kids love seeing their teachers and principals come into *their* neighborhood," Julia says.

And Julia loves to see a wide variety of people become involved with the Center and its kids. "Every time another person sits down with the children, the kids are learning *life* skills. Not just book skills. These kids are as smart and capable as any

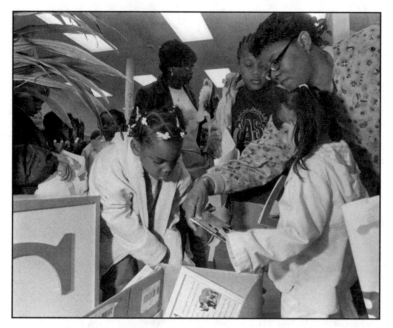

One of Julia's greatest joys is seeing children pick out books to take home.

other children, but they can't aspire to be something that they've never seen."

She explains by giving an example. "When I was a kid, all I knew about newspaper photographers was that when there was a homicide in the neighborhood, a photographer was behind that yellow tape where we weren't allowed to be. But the very first guest reader we had here was Mark Hertzberg, the head photographer from the Racine newspaper. He read the book *Goodnight, Moon*. The kids could see him and talk to him and realize that yes, he's a real person, a dad and a husband and a human being who also happens to be a newspaper photographer. And now they can think, 'Hey, maybe I'd like to be a photographer' instead of 'maybe I'll be a drug dealer.' Because before, dealing drugs might have been the only 'career' they really knew about."

Other "life skills" are taught as the need comes up. At one point, Julia suggested that some of the older students do an activity that involved reading a newspaper. The kids seemed reluctant, and Julia was puzzled. Then she realized the problem: they didn't understand *how* to read a newspaper. Their families were too poor to subscribe to a paper, and they had never learned to use one.

"You know how a story will skip from one page to another?" she says. "For instance, at the bottom of a column it might say, 'LIBRARY, sec. B, p. 3.' The kids didn't understand what that meant, or how to find the rest of the story. These were big kids—seventh, eighth grade—and they were embarrassed." Julia adds, "I can't let myself cry in front of the children. But that day I came close." Julia quickly organized a class on how to read a newspaper, and the Racine paper now donates five copies to the center each day. Now the older children routinely keep up with the news. Other children, members of a book club, munch on pizza as they discuss a story they've all read. And every day, volunteers sit in rocking chairs and read stories aloud to any youngsters who want to listen. "I'm 51 years old, and it still hurts to remember that no one ever read to me," Julia says. "These children won't have to say that."

As Julia talks, those old memories keep surfacing: the books atop her family's refrigerator, the longing for someone to read to her. It seems that Julia can never quite forget the little girl that she once was.

"Every little girl that walks in here—she's me," Julia says today. "Every child living in a house without books—that's me too. There are none that are poorer than I was. One of my earliest goals was to own a bottle of Ivory Liquid. We washed our dishes with the same powdered detergent we washed our clothes with. When I first saw dishwashing liquid, I wanted that so bad!" Because it helps her understand and reach the children around her, Julia never tries to whitewash her own difficult past. "Some people, they get a bit of success, and they act like they never knew hard times," she says. "That's not what I'm about."

Instead, Julia says, "I tell the children, 'Maybe the phone and the lights have been cut off at your house. Maybe your parents are drinking and fighting. Maybe you're feeling inferior because your clothes are raggedy and your hair isn't combed right. Maybe your house is full of cockroaches. Maybe you and your brothers and sisters all have to sleep in one bed. That's okay. That's how Ms. Burney lived, too.' And the children say, 'Naaaw, you didn't!' So I show them a photograph I keep in my office." That photo shows Julia as a young girl, standing with her parents. The hem is hanging out of her dress, and her coat has lost all its buttons but one.

"They look at the picture, and I tell them, 'That's how I grew up. But what's important is that *now* I have my own house, and my own car, and a good job. Your job now is to think what *you* want when you grow up, and to go to school and get it.' Then we get paper out and write, 'When I grow up, I'm going to . . .' We get those hopes and dreams down on paper."

As great a success as the Reading Center is, Julia is never satisfied that she is doing enough. She is constantly thinking of ways to reach more children in need. And so on one recent evening, after a long day at the Center, she went to speak to a meeting of teenage moms in downtown Racine. These young girls' babies, she knew, were at risk for a tough time in life. She hoped to reach their parents with her message.

As she talked with this group of 16- and 17-year-old mothers, Julia showed a side of herself that was quite different than the gentle, motherly person she is at the Center. She was direct, even fierce in her message, which could be boiled down to this: "Make your child proud to say, 'That's my mother.'"

Julia shared her own experience as a single teenage mother. She told of her own financial and emotional struggles. She spoke of the terrible odds that face teenage parents. But then she pointed to her four successful, educated children: a dentist, a police officer, a businesswoman, and a soldier. The children of young mothers *can* make it, she said—*if* their mothers make them their number-one priority.

"You want the bottom line?" she said, raising her voice like a revival preacher. " 'Cause if you want

*As the children at Cops 'n Kids read, write, and work on projects,
Julia is never far away.*

me to sugar-coat it, I can go home right now. But
if you want it straight, here it is. Doing the right
thing is *hard*. If you're gonna be a true mom—not
just some teenager who had a baby, but a *mother*—
your days of living life for yourself are over. You
might tell me, 'But I'm just 16—I have the right to
have fun.' But I'm telling you, you stopped being

16 the day you decided to have this child.

"And that means you *can't* do what your friends do. You *can't* leave the baby with just anyone. You *can't* hang out at the bars and get high." And, she added, girls who are "true moms" will lose friends. "A real mother will not allow people to come to her house to drink and fight and smoke dope around her children. She takes a stand." It's a hard thing to do, she added, but it's right. "I'd take my children to see my family, but when the drinking would start, we'd be out of there. And I'd hear, 'Oh, there she is again, making her kids out to be better than anyone else!' But you know what? That was just too bad! Because raising my kids right was my priority—not pleasing my friends and family."

On and on Julia went. Her gospel-style delivery, combined with an occasional wisecrack thrown out with perfect comic timing, kept the girls spellbound. Her advice was direct and practical: Stay in school. If you've dropped out, go back. Be an involved parent in your children's school. Know your child's teachers. Don't deny your child the right to know his or her father. Don't dump the baby off on your own mother. Have consistent rules for your child. Have a bedtime and stick to it. Dress like a mother, not like a streetwalker. Carry yourself like a mother. If your child wants you to bake cookies for school, for heaven's sake, learn to bake cookies. Don't have men moving in and out of your bedroom. Don't let your children see a man hit you. If you don't have discipline in your own life, don't expect to be able to discipline your child.

And, of course, she ended with her favorite topic: reading. Pointing to a newborn in one young girl's arms, she said, "That child is not too young to be read to. No child is. Read to your kids. I've brought some books here to get you started."

Julia passed out the books. She gave each girl a card advertising the Cops 'n Kids Reading Center. She distributed hugs. "Bring your children to see

The warm, cozy reading center she dreamed of is now a reality. Every morning, Julia unlocks the door of Cops 'n Kids to the children of her community.

us," she said. And with that she was gone. That night, her prayers would include the mothers and babies in that room.

If you want to see one answer to Julia Burney's prayers, look no further than 8th and Villa Streets in Racine, Wisconsin. There stands a handsome brick building, bursting with books and cozy sofas, soft chairs, quilts to snuggle up with, crayons and paints and hugs and love, and—always—children. Children by the dozen come trooping into the reading center that they call "Ms. Burney's place." They run to her with their report cards, shyly hand her thank-you notes they have created for her, and ask her to read them a story. They never leave disappointed.

Twenty-four hours a day, the big plate-glass window at the front of the Center is brightly lit. It has been "adopted" by the local Barnes & Noble store, and it is always colorfully decorated with a display of books to suit the season: spring, Christmas, St. Patrick's Day, Halloween, autumn. In the darkness of inner-city Racine, that window glows like a beacon, a symbol of Julia Burney's loving commitment to the children of her city.

In February 2001, after twenty-two years of service, Julia retired from the police force. She proudly turned her badge over to her daughter, Vanessa, who has become a Racine police officer herself. She now devotes all of her time and energy to the Cops 'n Kids Reading Center.

Julia tells whoever asks that she is repaying the debt she owes to her beloved aunt. "I believe in these children, because Aunt Ruby believed in me," she says. "I may not be around when these children are adults. But I know I've passed on the help I received. I'm just doing what I would want done for me."

A Special Offer

If you enjoyed this book, Townsend Press

has a special offer for you.

Turn the page to learn how to obtain five

entertaining, readable books

free of charge

except for shipping and handling.

Why Become a Regular Reader?

Many people believe that reading is the very heart of education. Here is what they say:

1. Reading provides language power. Research has shown beyond question that frequent reading improves vocabulary, spelling, grammar, writing style, and reading speed and comprehension. If you become a regular reader, all of these language and thinking abilities develop almost automatically!

2. Reading increases the chances for job success. In today's world more than ever, jobs involve processing information, with words being the tools of the trade. Studies have found that the better your command of words, the more success you are likely to experience. *Nothing gives you a command of words like regular reading.*

3. Reading creates human power. Reading enlarges the mind and the heart. It frees us from the narrow confines of our own experience. Knowing how other people view important matters helps us decide what we ourselves think and feel. Reading also helps us connect with others and realize our shared humanity. Someone once wrote, "We read in order to know that we are not alone." We become less isolated as we share the common experiences, emotions, and thoughts that make us human. We grow more sympathetic and kind because we realize that others are like us.

And for many people, reading is a source of real pleasure, opening the door to a lifetime of pleasure and adventure. By taking the time to walk through that door, you too may find that one of the great experiences of life is the joy of reading for its own sake.

Regular reading can, in short, change your life. The more you read, the more you know. The more you know, the more you grow.

A Special Offer

To promote your reading growth, Townend Press will send you the following five books, edited for today's readers, at no charge except for shipping and handling.

Great Stories of Suspense & Adventure

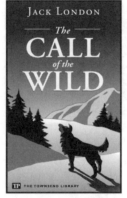

The Call of the Wild

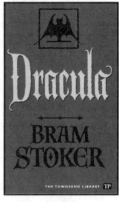

Dracula

The Jungle Book

White Fang

Use the order form on the next page. Enclose five dollars to cover the cost of shipping and handling. You will receive these five highly readable books plus a free copy of a booklet entitled *40 Good Books to Read*.

A Special Offer

Great Stories of
Suspense & Adventure

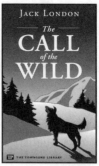

The Call of the Wild

The Jungle Book

White Fang

Dracula

Order Form

YES! Please send me copies of the five books shown.
Enclosed is five dollars to cover the shipping and handling.

Please PRINT very clearly. This will be your shipping label.

NAME _____

ADDRESS _____

CITY _____ STATE _____ ZIP _____

MAIL TO: TP Book Center
1038 Industrial Drive
West Berlin, NJ 08091